# Where do plants grow?

Louise and Richard Spilsbury

Heinemann
LIBRARY

young
Explorer

**www.heinemann.co.uk/library**
Visit our website to find out more information about Heinemann Library books.

To order:
 Phone 44 (0) 1865 888066
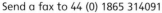 Send a fax to 44 (0) 1865 314091
 Visit the Heinemann Bookshop at www.heinemann.co.uk/library to browse our catalogue and order online.

First published in Great Britain by Heinemann Library,
Halley Court, Jordan Hill, Oxford
OX2 8EJ, part of Harcourt Education.
Heinemann is a registered trademark of Harcourt
Education Ltd.

Editorial: Kate Bellamy
Design: Jo Hinton-Malivoire and AMR
Illustration: Art Construction
Picture Research: Ruth Blair and Kay Altwegg
Production: Severine Ribierre

Originated by Repro Multi Warna
Printed and bound in China by South China Printing
Company

The paper used to print this book comes from
sustainable resources

ISBN 0 431 01805 7
10 09 08 07 06
10 9 8 7 6 5 4 3 2 1

**British Library Cataloguing in Publication Data**
Splisbury, Louise and Richard
Where do plants grow? – (World of plants)
581.7

A full catalogue record for this book is available from
the British Library.

**Acknowledgements**
The Publishers would like to thank the following for
permission to reproduce photographs: Alamy pp. **19**
(Agence Images), **6-7** (David R. Frazier Photolibrary, Inc.),
**20** (Tim Graham), **16** (George and Monserrate Schwartz),
**12** (Worldwide Picture Library); Corbis pp. **4a, 4b, 5a, 5b,
24, 25, 30b**; FLPA/Minden Pictures pp. **6** (Jim
Brandenburg), **27** (Konrad Wothe); Getty Images pp. **4,
11, 21, 26, 30a, 30c** (Photodisc); Harcourt Education pp.
**28, 29a, 29b** (Tudor photography); Naturepl.com pp. **15**
(Niall Benvie), **23** (Pete Cairns), **14** (Chris Gomersall), **8**
(Neil Lucas), **10** (Claudio Velasquez), **13** (Stefan
Wildstrand), **9, 22**.

Cover photograph of desert plants growing in sand,
New Mexico, USA, reproduced with permission of Corbis.

Our thanks to Patsy Dyer for her assistance in the
preparation of this book.

 **Find out more about plants at
www.heinemannexplore.co.uk**

# Contents

Words appearing in the text in bold, **like this**, are explained in the Glossary.

# Where do plants grow?

Plants grow all over the world. They grow near the sea, in deserts and even up mountains!

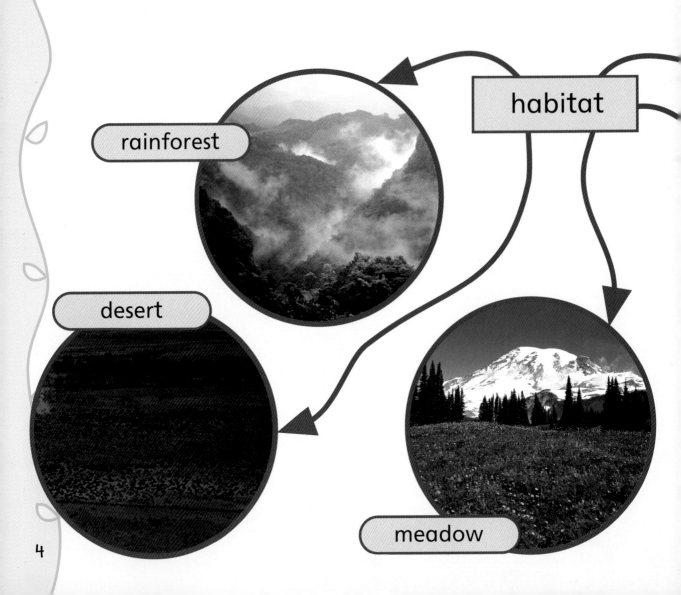

rainforest

habitat

desert

meadow

Different plants need different amounts of light, water, and warmth to grow well. The kind of place where a group of plants lives and grows is called a **habitat**.

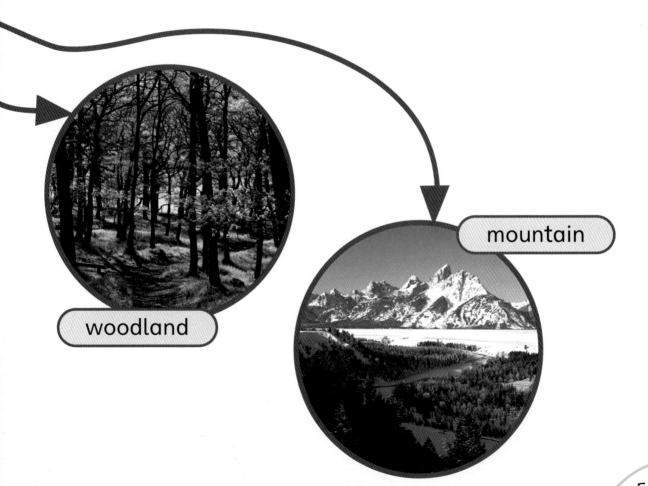

woodland

mountain

# Grassland

Flat areas covered mostly in grass are called grasslands. These **habitats** are warm and sunny and get quite a lot of rain.

American grassland is called prairie. The tallest prairie grasses can grow as high as a basketball hoop!

Grass **roots** spread through the **soil** and tangle together. New grass plants grow quickly from these roots. Grasses stop other plants growing because they grow quickly and take up so much space.

# Scrubland

Some hot **habitats** only have a little rain each year. They get just enough rain for a few trees and other plants to grow. These habitats are called scrubland.

This scrubland in Australia is on fire.

In dry summers scrubland plants may catch fire. The **stems** and leaves above the ground are burnt, but the **roots** deep underground are safe. New stems and leaves grow from the roots.

After a fire scrubland plants start to grow again!

# Hot, dry deserts

Deserts are hot, dry **habitats** that have very little rain. Desert plants have special ways of storing water. This keeps them alive when there is no rain.

Many desert plants have **stems** that get fatter so they can fill up with water.

Cactus plants have lots of spikes on their stems. These spikes are special leaves. They stop thirsty animals from biting the stems and drinking the water stored inside.

The spines on this cactus are very sharp!

# Rainforests

Forests that grow in very hot, rainy places are called rainforests. Rainforest trees get lots of water and sunlight so they grow very fast and very tall.

Some tall rainforest trees have very big **roots** that help to hold them up.

Big rainforest trees stop sunlight getting to the plants growing below them. Some plants grow up towards the sunlight by growing up the tree **trunks**.

# Broadleaf woodland

Woods where oak and beech trees grow are called broadleaf woodlands. Broadleaf woodland grows in damp places that have warm summers and cool winters.

Broadleaf trees have broad, flat leaves.

In autumn broadleaf trees lose all their leaves. Sunlight can get to the ground now there are no leaves in the way. Small plants start to grow. In spring the trees grow new leaves.

In spring, small plants cover the woodland floor with flowers.

15

# Conifer woodland

Woods with pine trees and fir trees are called conifer woodlands. Conifer woodlands grow in cold places. Most conifer trees have long, thin leaves. These leaves do not get hurt by snow and ice.

Conifer trees do not lose all their leaves in winter.

Conifer trees have leaves all year round. There is never much light for plants to grow on the ground under the trees.

Fern plants may grow in gaps between the trees where the sun can reach the ground.

# Cold, dry places

Only a few small plants grow at the tops of mountains and other cold, dry **habitats**. Some survive by growing close to the ground or in cracks in the rocks.

Mountain plants stay small to keep out of the way of cold winds.

Some small plants in cold habitats have furry leaves and **stems**. The hairs trap a layer of warm air next to the plant. This keeps the plant warm when the air all around is cold.

These flowers have furry **petals** to keep the plant warm in snowy places.

# Rivers and ponds

Plants that grow in rivers and ponds get plenty of water, but it can be dark underwater. Plants in these **habitats** have different ways of getting the sunlight they need.

Some river plants grow in the damp **soil** along the edge.

Some water plants have stiff **stems** to hold their leaves up. Others float on top of the water to get sunlight. They have big, round floating leaves.

Some plants, such as this water lily, cover the surface of ponds.

# Coasts

Coast **habitats** are where the land and sea meet. Seaweed is like a plant. It grows in the sea at the coast. Seaweed is tough and slimy so that waves do not damage it.

Seaweeds have parts called holdfasts that grip onto rocks to stop waves washing them away.

Seaweed has special leaves called **fronds**. Fronds help seaweed float near the surface of the water. By floating on the water they can get the sunlight that they need to grow.

Seaweed has air in its fronds. This helps it to float.

# Fields and farms

Farmers around the world grow plants that people can eat. They plant **seeds** in fields and help the plants grow by watering them.

These are huge fields of wheat. People use wheat to make flour for bread or pasta.

Tomatoes and some other food plants grow best in warm, sunny places. In cooler places, people grow tomatoes in greenhouses. Greenhouses trap warmth from the Sun.

The warm air inside this greenhouse helps the tomatoes grow.

# Towns and cities

In town and city **habitats** many plants grow in parks and gardens. People like to look at colourful plants. They plant **seeds** and choose where to grow the plants.

When land is left alone, **seeds** from wild plants blow onto the ground and start to grow. These unwanted plants are called weeds. Some land in towns is covered with weeds.

Dandelions and nettles are some of the weeds that grow in towns and cities.

# Try it yourself!

What happens when plants do not get enough water?

- Find two plants that are the same kind.

- Put them in a sunny place for ten days.

- Water one plant each day.

- Do not water the other plant.

What do you think will happen?

The plant that does not get watered turns brown and dies.

What if plants do not get light?

- Put one plant in a sunny place.

- Put the other plant in a dark place.

The plant in the dark place should go pale. It might even die.

- Water the plants every day.

What do you think will happen?

# Amazing plants!

Plants live all over the world!

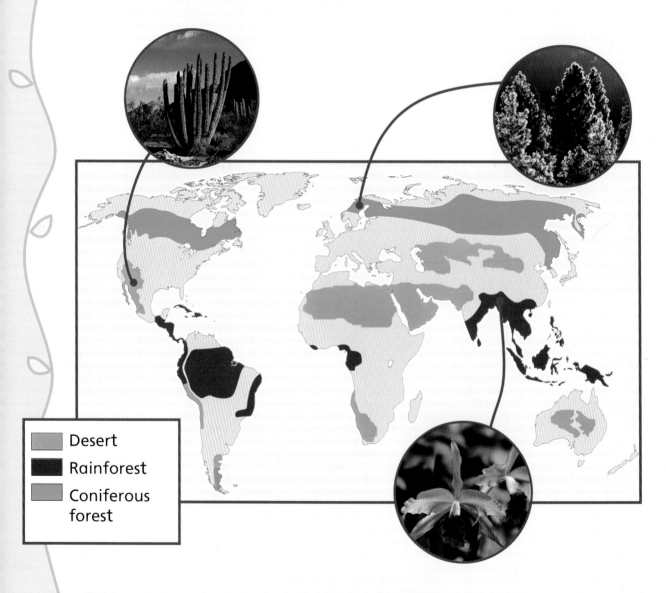

Desert

Rainforest

Coniferous forest

 Find out more about plants at
www.heinemannexplore.co.uk

# Glossary

**frond**  part of seaweed that looks like leaves

**habitat**  kind of place where a certain group of plants and animals live

**petal**  part of a flower

**root**  plant part that grows underground and takes in water from the soil

**seed**  plant part made by flowers. Seeds can grow to make a new plant.

**soil**  earth that plants grow in

**stem**  plant part that holds up leaves and flowers

**trunk**  large woody stem of a tree

# More books to read

*Habitat Explorer: Desert Explorer*, Greg Pyers (Raintree, 2004)

*Nature's Patterns: Season to Season*, Anita Ganeri (Heinemann, 2005)

*Read and Learn: Leaves*, Patricia Whitehouse (Raintree, 2004)

*The World Around Us: What is a forest?*, Monica Hughes (Raintree, 2004)

# Index

# Titles in the **_World of Plants_** series include:

Hardback           0 431 01804 9

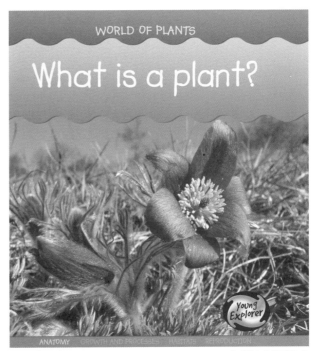

Hardback           0 431 01803 0

Hardback           0 431 01805 7

Hardback           0 431 01806 5

Find out about other titles from Heinemann Library on our website www.heinemann.co.uk/library